Jim and the Ants

Jim
and
the
Ants

A TRUE TALE, AS TOLD BY
QIGONG MASTER JIM NANCE

Written and illustrated by N.J. Nance

Guiding Qi LLC

Printed in the United States of America.

ISBN-13: 978-8-9914368-1-6

Published by Guiding Qi LLC 2025
www.guidingqi.com

Qi (chee) = energy

gong = to study

Qigong = to study energy

One early morning Jim sat on the floor the same way he sat every morning. With legs crossed and eyes closed he practiced Qigong meditation. He was completely still.

In his mind he pictured everything surrounded by a bright, beautiful light.

The light filled up his heart, his whole body, and it filled the room!

It was wonderful to be alive!

1

As he finished with the meditation he looked around at his big, empty house. Something was missing. There was one chair, one bed, one bowl and spoon... but not a sound.

There was no one to share a cup of tea with. Wind rattled at the window and Jim wondered if he would always be alone.

Just then a clear voice called out, "What about us? We've always been here." The voice was very near.

Jim looked to the right; he looked to the left.

Down on the floor he saw...

...one

ant

staring

up

at

him.

There were more.

Ants were on the rug, ants were on the chair; they were everywhere!

Now it's time to start paying close attention, thought Jim. *These ants may have something to say.*

There were big ones,

little ones,

strong ones,

gentle ones,

ants in a hurry,

10

ants who would

rather play,

day-dreamer ants,

and ants who

liked to put

things in

their place.

If a storm was approaching the ants would scurry around in a wild, electric dance!

Jim knew that someone was about to knock when the ants ran to the front door.

And as he left the house, they waited to see him off. When he returned, there they were, ready to greet him.

Jim studied the ants for three years.

He knew that if he studied something for a long time, amazing things would happen... .

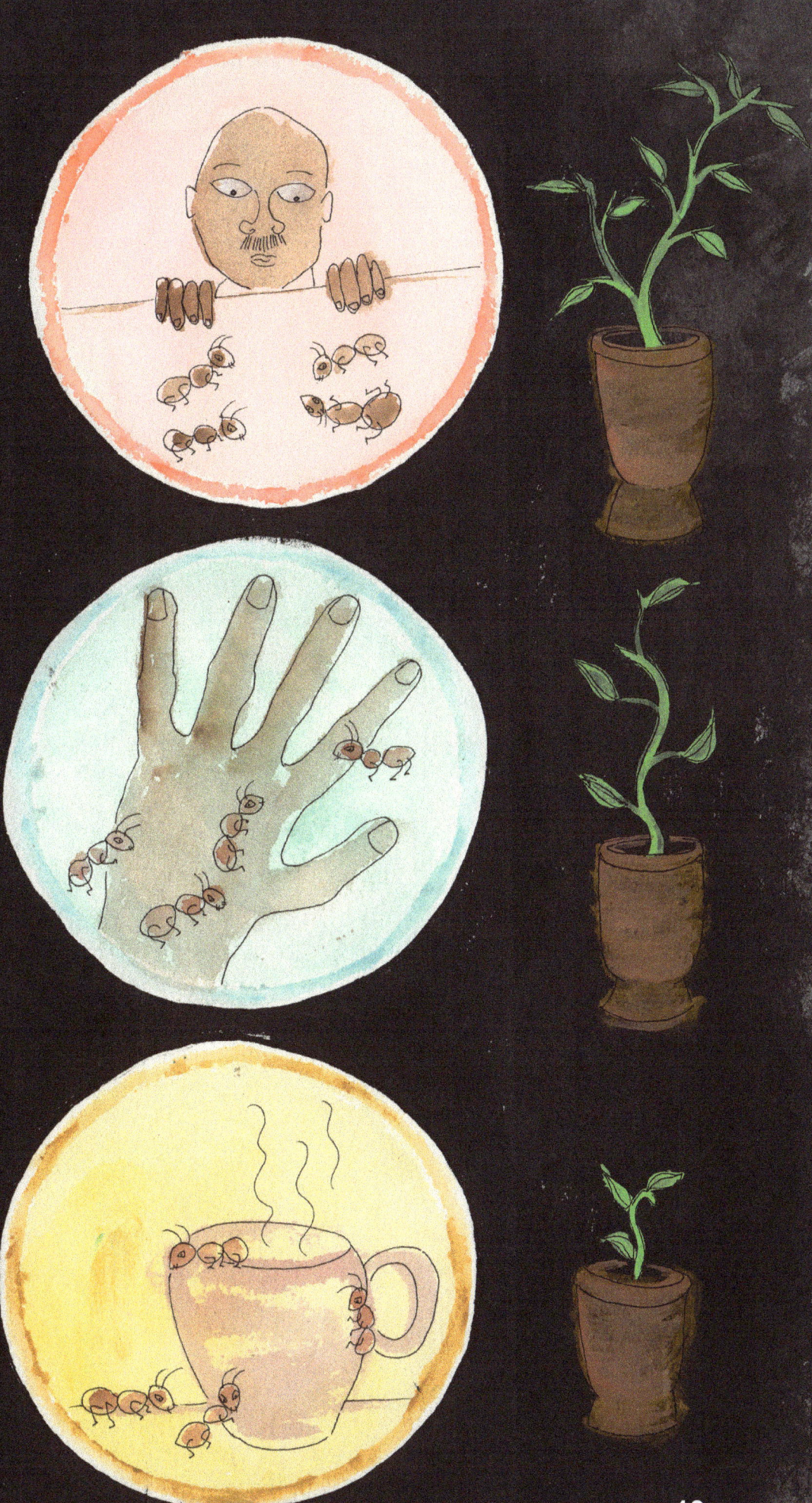

Every day Jim spent time with the ants. Every day he practiced meditation.

Always a few ants joined him.

As he sat with his legs crossed, the ants gathered just below each knee.

Together they were very still.

Jim closed his eyes and took a deep breath. In his mind he saw a great golden sun standing right in front of them.

"Hello, Sun. Thank you for joining us!"

Warm rays streamed down; they were surrounded by bright, beautiful light!

It seemed as though Jim and the ants were made completely of light!

It was so peaceful.

After the meditation the ants went their own way, crossing the floor once more.

"Please come again friends!" said Jim.

One afternoon sleep crept over Jim.

"One minute, maybe two... . I'm going to lie down right here... ."

Jim headed to the floor with a yawn.

Just then he saw Mother Ant. She raced back and forth trying to tell him something.

But Jim's eyes were heavy and his body soft.

He fell to the floor in a deep sleep heap.

17

Moments later, Jim's eyes opened to find Mother Ant, and now Father Ant, too.

In a jig-jagged way they jetted about!

"Oh no! Something must be very wrong!" cried Jim.

Jim gasped.

There was Baby Ant, crumpled and still.

He had squashed the little ant!

Mother Ant had tried to warn him. If only he would've listened more carefully!

She stood holding the little one.

"Please help!"

Then, without pause, Father Ant climbed up Jim's body; as if he were climbing a mountain!

He went all the way to the top and perched there on Jim's head.

So, with one ant up top, and two down below, Jim sent healing energy to the little ant.

The energy moved through his hands, and then through the body of Baby Ant.

The ant was glowing with light!

28

But Baby Ant still did not move.

"I'm so sorry," he said to the ants, "For now I've done all that I can do.

"I will keep working to send more healing energy to the little one."

Father Ant climbed down from Jim's head. He and Mother Ant carried Baby Ant away.

Jim's heart felt heavy, as though a great weight were pressing down on his chest.

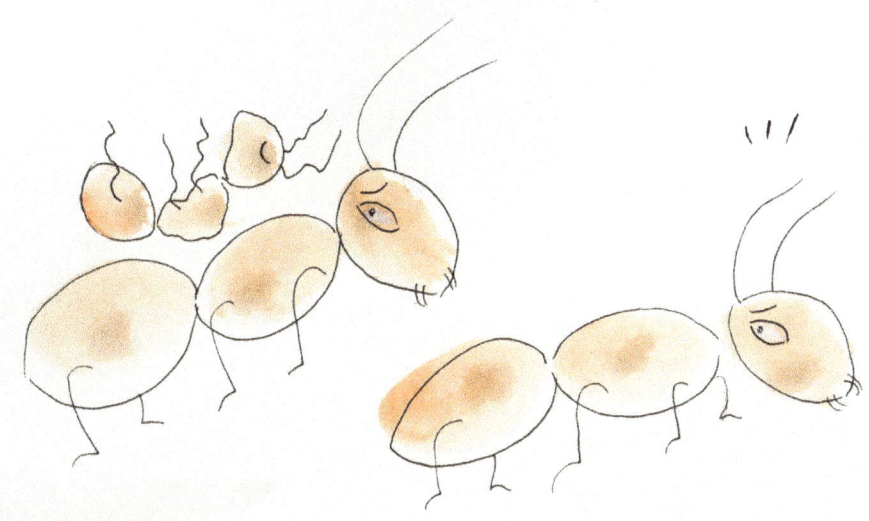

The next day, Jim was still thinking of Baby Ant.

The big house was quiet and empty.

He was alone.

Remembering all of the wonderful times he had with the ants, he was so grateful to know them.

The sun rose and filled the house with a light so bright, it seemed as if the whole house were sitting in the center of the sun!

And then he noticed he wasn't alone.

"It's a miracle!" Jim cried out.

There was Mother Ant, Father Ant, and...
Baby Ant! Completely healed!

Jim laughed such a mighty laugh, the walls
shook as if they were laughing, too!

It was time for a celebration.

Jim went out into the world to find the perfect thing.

And he knew just what to get.

When he returned home,

the ants were waiting on the kitchen counter.

He offered them a little piece of cantaloupe.

"Now, how about just a little bit more?" said
Father Ant.

"Of course!" Jim cut a large slice. "It's for everyone!"

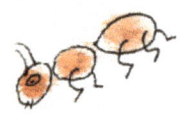

Ants told ant friends, friends
told neighbors,

and neighbors told more
friends, until it became...

...an ant party!

43

By the time Jim was ready to leave,

ants were streaming into the house!

In the morning there was no melon left. All of the ants had disappeared.

All except four, who stood in the middle of the living room floor; Mother Ant, and three new little ants.

"Thank you, my friend," she said.

"Thank you, all," replied Jim. "Thank you for everything."

Then, just as he did every morning, Jim crossed his legs and closed his eyes to practice meditation.

The ants came over and settled in, just beneath his knees.

As golden morning light filled the house, Jim and the ants sat together once more.

The End

I feel honored to share this experience with anyone interested in listening. I hope that everyone may have an opportunity to study another life form, and as a result have a deeper understanding of themselves.

–Master Jim Nance

THE SCIENCE OF QIGONG

Qigong (pronounced chee-gung) means "to study energy." The practice of Qigong is an ancient science and discipline that originated over seven thousand years ago in China and often incorporates variations of meditation, movement, and sound. Today, people practice Qigong all around the world.

Medical Qigong is the study and practice of using energy for healing purposes. Intelligent energy (Qi) consistently flows throughout the body; blockages in this energetic system can cause pain, discomfort, or even illness. Practicing Qigong can help improve the flow of energy in ourselves, in other people, in animals, and even in places and things. When Qi is running smoothly, we can experience an optimal state of health and happiness. There are many different forms of Qigong in the world; Master Jim Nance practices Spring Forest Qigong.

ABOUT MASTER JIM NANCE

Sidney James (Jim) Nance is a Qigong Master and Educator. He earned a B.A. in Elementary Education from Antioch College and a M.S. in Career & Academic Counseling from North Carolina Central University. He has worked with inner-city youth in Philadelphia, Houston, Cincinnati, and extensively in the Minneapolis Public Schools.

After twenty-seven years of searching for a Qigong Master, he met Chunyi Lin, an extraordinary Master from China. In 1995, he began learning Qigong through Master Lin. After practicing and studying, Jim became a healer and instructor at the Spring Forest Qigong Healing Center in Minnesota and was named the first Spring Forest Qigong Master (2005). He continued to work as a healer at the SFQ Healing center until retirement (2014). Day to day, Master Jim Nance cultivates his Qigong practice and refines his healing technique while continuing to work to bring healing energy to people around the world. He can be contacted for healing services, as well as written and audio materials through his website www.guidingqi.com

AUTHOR AND ILLUSTRATOR N.J.NANCE

As a young child, Naomi was always attempting to heal animals, insects, and even her dolls. Healing became a reality when she discovered Spring Forest Qigong (2005). When Jim proposed the work for this book, she knew immediately that it was the right thing to do. Naomi is a multidisciplinary artist working in the areas of performance art (music, theater, dance), visual art, design, and writing over the past two decades. She continues to practice Qigong, paint, and create books. You can learn more about her work at www.naomijoynance.com.

THE SCIENTIST AND THE WRITER

BY N.J. NANCE

Thank You

For this project, we'd like to thank Chunyi Lin, everyone who heard the story and encouraged us along the way, our editor Charlotte Sullivan, and of course, the ants.